Scripture Scr

Primary
Volume IV

Practicing Proverbs

(Especially for Lefties)

CONCEIVED & WRITTEN BY
Mary Ellen Tedrow-Wynn

COVER, LAYOUT DESIGN, & TYPESETTING BY
Allison Armerding

Dedication

The is dedicated to my special "lefty" little brother Christopher,
and to my lefty sons, Adam and Micah.
Thank you, "Little Brother," for your part in my life.
Thank you, Adam, for loving me all the time.
Thank you, Micah, for touching my life and supporting me through tough times.
Each of you are special to me beyond words. May all of you be blessed.

Also, to all the lefties who will use this book:
I pray that God will use these Scriptures to mold your lives.
Read them, trace them, and copy them. But most of all, hide them . . . in your heart.

Copyright

Scripture Scribes: Practicing Proverbs
Laurelwood Books © 2016
ISBN: 978-1-941383-30-8

We have checked for errors in this text. However, should you notice any mistakes, we would love to hear from you.
Please contact us at *marylnw7@gmail.com*

Scripture quotations marked "KJV" are taken from The King James Bible. Public Domain.

Scripture quotations marked "ESV" are taken from The Holy Bible, English Standard Version.
Copyright © 2000; 2001 by Crossway Bibles, a division of Good News Publishers.
Used by permission. All rights reserved.

Scripture quotations marked "NIV" are taken from the Holy Bible, New International Version®. NIV®.
Copyright © 1973, 1978, 1984 by International Bible Society. Used by permission of Zondervan. All rights reserved.

Scripture quotations marked "NKJV" are taken from the New King James Version.
Copyright © 1982 by Thomas Nelson, Inc. Used by permission. All rights reserved.

Not to be reproduced without express written permission from the publisher. Thank you for respecting this.
Schools and/or co-ops, please contact us for group discounts.

Find this and other great books on our website:
www.laurelwoodbooks.com
You may also reach us at:
Laurelwood Books
1639 Ebenezer Road
Bluemont, VA 20135

Scripture Scribes

Scripture Scribes is copy work for students to write and fall in love with the Scriptures.

Scripture Scribes: Practicing Proverbs features:

- 30 week-long lessons using several English translations of the Bible
- Reading Scripture
- Tracing Scripture
- Copying Scripture

Lesson 1: Day 1

Trace and Copy Key Words

subtilty
knowledge
discretion

To give subtilty to the simple,
to the young man knowledge and discretion.

Proverbs 1:4 KJV

Trace and copy the verse below.

To give subtilty to the simple,

to the young man knowledge and

discretion.

Lesson 1: Day 2

Trace and Copy Key Words

learning
understanding
counsels

A wise man will hear, and will increase learning;
and a man of understanding shall attain unto wise counsels:

Proverbs 1:5 KJV

Trace and copy the verse below.

A wise man will hear,

and a man of understanding learning

shall attain unto wise counsels

Practicing Proverbs © 2016 Not to be reproduced.

Lesson 1: Day 3

The fear of the LORD is the beginning of knowledge:

but fools despise wisdom and instruction.

Proverbs 1:7 KJV

Trace and Copy Key Words

beginning
wisdom
instruction

Trace and copy the verse below.

The fear of the LORD is the

beginning of knowledge: but

fools despise wisdom and instruction.

Lesson 1: Day 4

My son, hear the instruction of thy father,

and forsake not the law of thy mother:

Proverbs 1:8 KJV

Trace and Copy Key Words

father

forsake

mother

Trace and copy the verse below.

My son, hear the instruction of thy father,

and forsake not the law of thy mother:

My son, hear the instruction of thy father,

and forsake not the law of thy mother:

Practicing Proverbs © 2016 Not to be reproduced.

Lesson 2: Day 1

My son, if sinners entice you,

Do not consent.

Proverbs 1:10 NKJV

Trace and Copy Key Words

sinners

entice

consent

Trace and copy the verse below.

My son,

if sinners entice you,

Do not consent.

Lesson 2: Day 2

Trace and Copy Key Words

greedy

gain

owners

So are the ways of everyone who is greedy for gain;

It takes away the life of its owners.

Proverbs 1:19 NKJV

Trace and copy the verse below.

So are the ways of everyone

who is greedy for gain.

It takes away the life

of its owners.

Lesson 2: Day 3

> "But whoever listens to me will dwell safely,
> And will be secure, without fear of evil."
>
> Proverbs 1:33 NKJV

Trace and Copy Key Words

dwell
safely
secure

Trace and copy the verse below.

"But whoever listens to me will dwell safely,

And will be secure, without fear of evil."

Lesson 2: Day 4

For the LORD gives wisdom;

From His mouth come knowledge and understanding;

Proverbs 2:6 NKJV

Trace and Copy Key Words

wisdom

mouth

knowledge

Trace and copy the verse below.

For the LORD gives wisdom;

from His mouth come knowledge and understanding.

For the LORD gives wisdom;

from His mouth come knowledge and understanding.

Lesson 3: Day 1

He holds success in store for the upright,

he is a shield to those whose walk is blameless,

Proverbs 2:7 NIV

Trace and Copy Key Words

upright
a
blameless

Trace and copy the verse below.

He holds success in store for the upright,

he is a shield to those whose walk is blameless,

Lesson 3: Day 2

For wisdom will enter your heart,

and knowledge will be pleasant to your soul.

Proverbs 2:10 NIV

Trace and Copy Key Words

heart

pleasant

soul

Trace and copy the verse below.

For wisdom will enter your heart,

and be pleasant to your soul.

For wisdom will enter your heart,

and be pleasant to your soul.

Lesson 3: Day 3

**Discretion will protect you,
and understanding will guard you.
Proverbs 2:11 NIV**

Trace and Copy Key Words

discretion
protect
guard

Trace and copy the verse below.

Discretion will protect you,

and understanding will guard you.

Lesson 3: Day 4

For the upright will live in the land,

and the blameless will remain in it;

Proverbs 2:21 NIV

Trace and Copy Key Words

upright

blameless

remain

Trace and copy the verse below.

For the upright will live in the land,

and the blameless will remain in it;

For the upright will live in the land,

and the blameless will remain in it;

Lesson 4: Day 1

My son, do not forget my teaching,
but let your heart keep my commandments,

Proverbs 3:1 ESV

Trace and Copy Key Words

forget

teaching

commandments

Trace and copy the verse below.

My son, do not forget my teaching,

but let your heart keep my

commandments, but let your

heart keep my commandments,

Lesson 4: Day 2

Trace and Copy Key Words

length
years
peace

for length of days and years of life

and peace they will add to you.

Proverbs 3:1 ESV

Trace and copy the verse below.

for length of days and years of life

and peace they will add to you.

for length of days and years of life

and peace they will add to you.

Lesson 4: Day 3

Let not steadfast love and faithfulness forsake you;
bind them around your neck;
write them on the tablet of your heart.

Proverbs 3:3 ESV

Trace and Copy Key Words

steadfast
forsake
tablet

Trace and copy the verse below.

Let not steadfast love

and faithfulness forsake

them them around your neck

write them on the tablet of your heart.

Lesson 4: Day 4

So you will find favor and good success

in the sight of God and man.

Proverbs 3:4 ESV

Trace and Copy Key Words

favor

good

sight

Trace and copy the verse below.

So you will find favor and good success

in the sight of God and man.

So you will find favor and good success

in the sight of God and man.

Lesson 5: Day 1

Trust in the LORD with all thine heart;

and lean not unto thine own understanding.

Proverbs 3:5 KJV

Trace and Copy Key Words

trust

the

lean

Trace and copy the verse below.

Trust in the LORD

with all thine heart;

and lean not unto

thine own understanding.

Lesson 5: Day 2

In all thy ways acknowledge him,

and he shall direct thy paths.

Proverbs 3:6 KJV

Trace and Copy Key Words

acknowledge

direct

paths

Trace and copy the verse below.

In all thy ways acknowledge him,

and he shall direct thy paths.

In all thy ways acknowledge him,

and he shall direct thy paths.

Lesson 5: Day 3

Be not wise in thine own eyes:

fear the LORD, and depart from evil.

Proverbs 3:7 KJV

Trace and Copy Key Words

wise

fear

depart

Trace and copy the verse below.

Be not wise in thine own eyes:

fear the LORD, and depart from evil.

Lesson 5: Day 4

It shall be health to thy navel,

and marrow to thy bones.

Proverbs 3:8 ESV

Trace and Copy Key Words

health

marrow

Proverbs

Trace and copy the verse below.

It shall be health to thy navel,

and marrow to thy bones.

It shall be health to thy navel,

and marrow to thy bones.

Lesson 6: Day 1

Honor the LORD with your possessions,
And with the firstfruits of all your increase;

Proverbs 3:9 NKJV

Trace and Copy Key Words

honor
possessions
firstfruits

Trace and copy the verse below.

Honor the LORD with your possessions,
and with the firstfruits of all your increase;

Lesson 6: Day 2

So your barns will be filled with plenty,

And your vats will overflow with new wine.

Proverbs 3:10 NKJV

Trace and Copy Key Words

plenty

vats

overflow

Trace and copy the verse below.

So your barns will be filled with plenty,

And your vats will overflow with new wine.

Lesson 6: Day 3

My son, do not despise the chastening of the LORD,

Nor detest His correction;

Proverbs 3:11 NKJV

Trace and Copy Key Words

chastening

detest

correction

Trace and copy the verse below.

My son, do not despise

the chastening

of the LORD,

nor detest His correction;

Lesson 6: Day 4

For whom the LORD loves He corrects,

Just as a father the son in whom he delights.

Proverbs 3:12 NKJV

Trace and Copy Key Words

loves

father

delights

Trace and copy the verse below.

For whom the LORD loves He corrects,

Just as a father the son in whom he delights.

For whom the LORD loves He corrects,

Just as a father the son in whom he delights.

Lesson 7: Day 1

My son, do not let wisdom and understanding out of your sight,

preserve sound judgment and discretion;

Proverbs 3:21 NIV

Trace and Copy Key Words

preserve

sound

judgment

Trace and copy the verse below.

My son, do not let

wisdom and

understanding out of your sight,

preserve sound judgment

and discretion;

Lesson 7: Day 2

Have no fear of sudden disaster
or of the ruin that overtakes the wicked,

Proverbs 1:5 KJV

Trace and Copy Key Words

builders
disaster
ruin

Trace and copy the verse below.

Have no fear of sudden disaster

or of the ruin that overtakes the wicked,

Lesson 7: Day 3

for the LORD will be at your side
and will keep your foot from being snared.

Proverbs 3:26 NIV

Trace and Copy Key Words

will
foot
snared

Trace and copy the verse below.

for the LORD will be at your side

and will keep your foot from

being snared.

Lesson 7: Day 4

Do not withhold good from those to whom it is due,

when it is in your power to act.

Proverbs 3:27 NIV

Trace and Copy Key Words

withhold

due

power

Trace and copy the verse below.

Do not withhold good

from those to whom it is due,

when it is in

your power to act.

Lesson 8: Day 1

The wise will inherit honor,
but fools get disgrace.
Proverbs 3:35 ESV

Trace and Copy Key Words

inherit
fools
disgrace

Trace and copy the verse below.

The wise will inherit honor,
but fools get disgrace.

Lesson 8: Day 2

Hear, O sons, a father's instruction,

and be attentive, that you may gain insight,

Proverbs 4:1 ESV

Trace and Copy Key Words

instruction

attentive

insight

Trace and copy the verse below.

Hear, O sons, a father's instruction,

and be attentive, that you may gain insight,

Hear, O sons, a father's instruction,

and be attentive, that you may gain insight,

Lesson 8: Day 3

> The beginning of wisdom is this: Get wisdom,
> and whatever you get, get insight.
>
> Proverbs 4:7 ESV

Trace and Copy Key Words

beginning
wisdom
insight

Trace and copy the verse below.

The beginning of wisdom is this: Get

wisdom, and whatever you get, get

insight.

Lesson 8: Day 4

Hear, my son, and accept my words,

that the years of your life may be many.

Proverbs 4:10 ESV

Trace and Copy Key Words

accept

words

years

Trace and copy the verse below.

Hear, my son, and accept my words,

that the years of life may be many,

Hear, my son, and accept my words,

that the years of life may be many,

Lesson 9: Day 1

Take fast hold of instruction; let her not go:

keep her; for she is thy life.

Proverbs 4:13 KJV

Trace and Copy Key Words

fast

let

instruction

Trace and copy the verse below.

Take fast hold of instruction; let her not go:

keep her; for she is thy life.

Lesson 9: Day 2

The way of the wicked is as darkness:

they know not at what they stumble.

Proverbs 4:19 KJV

Trace and Copy Key Words

wicked

darkness

stumble

Trace and copy the verse below.

The way of the wicked is as darkness:

they know not at what they stumble.

Lesson 9: Day 3

Let thine eyes look right on,
and let thine eyelids look straight before thee.

Proverbs 4:25 KJV

Trace and Copy Key Words

eyes

eyelids

straight

Trace and copy the verse below.

Let thine eyes look right on,

and let thine eyelids look straight before thee.

Lesson 9: Day 4

Turn not to the right hand nor to the left:

remove thy foot from evil.

Proverbs 4:27 KJV

Trace and Copy Key Words

turn

remove

evil

Trace and copy the verse below.

Turn not to the right hand nor to the left

remove thy foot from evil

Turn not to the right hand nor to the left

remove thy foot from evil

Lesson 10: Day 1

For the ways of man are before the eyes of the LORD,

And He ponders all his paths.

Proverbs 5:21 NKJV

Trace and Copy Key Words

ways

ponders

paths

Trace and copy the verse below.

For the ways of man

are before the eyes of the LORD,

And He ponders

all his paths.

Lesson 10: Day 2

Trace and Copy Key Words

ant

sluggard

consider

Go to the ant, you sluggard!

Consider her ways and be wise,

Proverbs 6:6 NKJV

Trace and copy the verse below.

Go to the ant, you sluggard;

consider her ways and be wise,

Lesson 10: Day 3

A little sleep, a little slumber,

A little folding of the hands to sleep—

Proverbs 6:10 NKJV

Trace and Copy Key Words

sleep

slumber

folding

Trace and copy the verse below.

A little sleep, a little slumber,

A little folding of the hands to sleep—

Lesson 10: Day 4

So shall your poverty come on you like a prowler,

And your need like an armed man.

Proverbs 6:11 NKJV

Trace and Copy Key Words

poverty

prowler

armed

Trace and copy the verse below.

So shall your poverty

come on you like a prowler,

And your need

like an armed man.

Bible History

The word "Bible" comes from the Greek work *biblia*, which means "books." The Bible is a collection of many books. It took many years--about 1100--to gather them all together in what we now call the Bible.

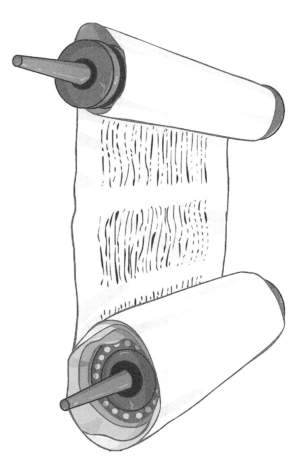

When the books were written, they did not have computers, or typewriters, or even paper as we do today. They had *papyrus*, a paper-like material made out of reeds, or dried animal skin called *vellum*. Can you imagine writing on such things? We are so accustomed to having lots of paper, it is hard for us to think about writing a book report or a whole book using only these materials.

Bible History

Oh, and they didn't have pens or pencils like we do. They had quills pens which were made from the feathers of birds. It probably sounds like a lot of fun but if you had to do it all the time for all your writing, you might get tired of it. Try finding a large feather, cutting the end off of the shaft, dipping it in ink and try writing like the scribes of old!

Lesson 11: Day 1

My son, keep your father's command
and do not forsake your mother's teaching.

Proverbs 6:20 NIV

Trace and Copy Key Words

command

keep

mother

Trace and copy the verse below.

My son, keep your father's command,

and do not forsake your mother's teaching.

Lesson 11: Day 2

Keep my commands and you will live;

guard my teachings as the apple of your eye.

Proverbs 7:2 NIV

Trace and Copy Key Words

commands

guard

apple

Trace and copy the verse below.

Keep my commands and you will live;

guard my teachings as the apple of your eye.

Lesson 11: Day 3

Now then, my sons, listen to me;
pay attention to what I say.
Proverbs 7:24 NIV

Trace and Copy Key Words

listen

attention

say

Trace and copy the verse below.

Now then, my sons, listen to me;

pay attention to what I say.

Lesson 11: Day 4

Does not wisdom call out?

Does not understanding raise her voice?

Proverbs 8:1 NIV

Trace and Copy Key Words

wisdom

raise

voice

Trace and copy the verse below.

Does not wisdom call out?

Does not wisdom call out?

Does not understanding raise her voice?

Does not understanding raise her voice?

Lesson 12: Day 1

Hear, for I will speak noble things,
and from my lips will come what is right,

Proverbs 8:6 ESV

Trace and Copy Key Words

noble
lips
right

Trace and copy the verse below.

Lesson 12: Day 2

Take my instruction instead of silver,

and knowledge rather than choice gold,

Proverbs 8:10 ESV

Trace and Copy Key Words

silver

choice

gold

Trace and copy the verse below.

Take my instruction rather than choice gold,

Take my instruction rather than choice gold,

Lesson 12: Day 3

for wisdom is better than jewels,

and all that you may desire cannot compare with her.

Proverbs 8:11 ESV

Trace and Copy Key Words

jewels

desire

compare

Trace and copy the verse below.

for wisdom

is better than jewels,

and that you may desire

cannot compare with her.

Lesson 12: Day 4

Trace and Copy Key Words

prudence
prudent
discretion

"I, wisdom, dwell with prudence,

and I find knowledge and discretion."

Proverbs 8:12 ESV

Trace and copy the verse below.

"I, wisdom, dwell with prudence,

and I find knowledge and discretion."

Lesson 13: Day 1

The fear of the LORD is to hate evil: pride, and arrogancy,

and the evil way, and the froward mouth, do I hate.

Proverbs 8:13 KJV

Trace and Copy Key Words

pride

arrogancy

froward

Trace and copy the verse below.

The fear of the LORD

is to hate evil: pride,

and arrogancy, and the

evil way, and the froward

mouth, do I hate.

Lesson 13: Day 2

I love them that love me;

and those that seek me early shall find me.

Proverbs 8:17 KJV

Trace and Copy Key Words

love

seek

early

Trace and copy the verse below.

I love them that love me;

and those that seek me early shall find me.

I love them that love me;

and those that seek me early shall find me.

Lesson 13: Day 3

Hear instruction, and be wise,

and refuse it not.

Proverbs 8:33 KJV

Trace and Copy Key Words

instruction

wise

refuse

Trace and copy the verse below.

Hear instruction, and be wise,

and refuse it not.

Lesson 13: Day 4

Trace and Copy Key Words

forsake
foolish
live

Forsake the foolish, and live;
and go in the way of understanding.
Proverbs 9:6 KJV

Trace and copy the verse below.

Forsake the foolish, and live, and go in the way of understanding.

Forsake the foolish, and live, and go in the way of understanding.

Lesson 14: Day 1

Give instruction to a wise man, and he will be still wiser;
Teach a just man, and he will increase in learning.

Proverbs 9:9 NKJV

Trace and Copy Key Words

wise

just

learning

Trace and copy the verse below.

Give instruction to a wise man,

and he will be still wiser;

Teach a just man,

and he will increase in learning.

Lesson 14: Day 2

The fear of the LORD is the beginning of wisdom,
And the knowledge of the Holy One is understanding.

Proverbs 9:10 NKJV

Trace and Copy Key Words

fear
LORD
Holy One

Trace and copy the verse below.

The fear of the LORD

is the beginning of wisdom,

And the knowledge of the Holy One

is understanding.

Practicing Proverbs © 2016 Not to be reproduced.

Lesson 14: Day 3

A wise son makes a glad father,

But a foolish son is the grief of his mother.

Proverbs 10:1 NKJV

Trace and Copy Key Words

wise

son

grief

Trace and copy the verse below.

A wise son makes a

glad father, but a foolish

son is the grief of his

mother.

Lesson 14: Day 4

He who has a slack hand becomes poor,

But the hand of the diligent makes rich.

Proverbs 10:4 NKJV

Trace and Copy Key Words

slack

hand

diligent

Trace and copy the verse below.

He who has a slack hand becomes poor,

But the hand of the diligent makes rich.

He who has a slack hand becomes poor,

But the hand of the diligent makes rich.

Lesson 15: Day 1

Blessings crown the head of the righteous,
but violence overwhelms the mouth of the wicked.

Proverbs 10:6 NIV

Trace and Copy Key Words

blessings
righteous
wicked

Trace and copy the verse below.

Blessings crown the head of the righteous

but violence overwhelms the mouth of the wicked

Lesson 15: Day 2

Whoever walks in integrity walks securely,

but whoever takes crooked paths will be found out.

Proverbs 10:9 NIV

Trace and Copy Key Words

integrity

securely

crooked

Trace and copy the verse below.

Whoever walks in integrity

takes crooked paths will be found out.

Whoever walks in integrity

takes crooked paths will be found out.

Lesson 15: Day 3

Hatred stirs up conflict,
but love covers over all wrongs.
Proverbs 10:12 NIV

Trace and Copy Key Words

hatred
conflict
wrongs

Trace and copy the verse below.

Hatred stirs up conflict,
but love covers over all
wrongs

Lesson 15: Day 4

The wages of the righteous is life,

but the earnings of the wicked are sin and death.

Proverbs 10:16 NIV

Trace and Copy Key Words

wages
earnings
death

Trace and copy the verse below.

The wages of the righteous is life,

but the earnings of the wicked are sin and death.

Lesson 16: Day 1

The lips of the righteous feed many,
but fools die for lack of sense.
Proverbs 10:21 ESV

Trace and Copy Key Words

lips
feed
sense

Trace and copy the verse below.

The lips of the righteous feed many,

but the lips of the righteous feed many,

but fools die for lack of sense.

Lesson 16: Day 2

Trace and Copy Key Words

vinegar
teeth
smoke

Like vinegar to the teeth and smoke to the eyes,

so is the sluggard to those who send him.

Proverbs 10:26 ESV

Trace and copy the verse below.

Like vinegar to the teeth and smoke to the eyes,

so is the sluggard to those who send him.

Lesson 16: Day 3

When pride comes, then comes disgrace,
but with the humble is wisdom.

Proverbs 11:2 ESV

Trace and Copy Key Words

pride
&
humble

Trace and copy the verse below.

When pride comes, then comes disgrace,

but with the humble is wisdom.

Lesson 16: Day 4

Whoever belittles his neighbor lacks sense,

but a man of understanding remains silent.

Proverbs 11:12 ESV

Trace and Copy Key Words

belittles

neighbor

silent

Trace and copy the verse below.

Whoever belittles his neighbor lacks sense,

but a man of understanding remains silent.

Whoever belittles his neighbor lacks sense,

but a man of understanding remains silent.

Lesson 17: Day 1

A talebearer revealeth secrets:

but he that is of a faithful spirit concealeth the matter.

Proverbs 11:13 KJV

Trace and Copy Key Words

talebearer

revealeth

concealeth

Trace and copy the verse below.

A talebearer

revealeth secrets:

but he that is of a faithful spirit

concealeth the matter.

Lesson 17: Day 2

He that diligently seeketh good procureth favour:

but he that seeketh mischief, it shall come unto him.

Proverbs 11:27 KJV

Trace and Copy Key Words

procureth

favour

mischief

Trace and copy the verse below.

He that diligently seeketh good

procureth favour

but he that seeketh mischief

it shall come unto him.

Lesson 17: Day 3

The fruit of the righteous is a tree of life;

and he that winneth souls is wise.

Proverbs 11:30 KJV

Trace and Copy Key Words

fruit

winneth

souls

Trace and copy the verse below.

The fruit of the righteous is a tree of life;

and he that winneth souls is wise.

Lesson 17: Day 4

Whoso loveth instruction loveth knowledge:

but he that hateth reproof is brutish.

Proverbs 12:1 KJV

Trace and Copy Key Words

loveth

hateth

brutish

Trace and copy the verse below.

Whoso loveth instruction loveth

he that hateth reproof is brutish.

Whoso loveth instruction loveth

he that hateth reproof is brutish.

Lesson 18: Day 1

A good man obtains favor from the LORD,

But a man of wicked intentions He will condemn.

Proverbs 12:2 NKJV

Trace and Copy Key Words

obtains

intentions

condemn

Trace and copy the verse below.

A good man obtains favor

from the LORD,

But a man of wicked intentions

He will condemn.

Lesson 18: Day 2

Trace and Copy Key Words

excellent

crown

rottenness

An excellent wife is the crown of her husband,

But she who causes shame is like rottenness in his bones.

Proverbs 12:4 NKJV

Trace and copy the verse below.

An excellent wife

Is the crown of her husband,

But she who causes shame

Is like rottenness in his bones.

Lesson 18: Day 3

A righteous man regards the life of his animal,

But the tender mercies of the wicked are cruel.

Proverbs 12:10 NKJV

Trace and Copy Key Words

animal

tender

mercies

Trace and copy the verse below.

A righteous man regards the life of his animal,

But the tender mercies of the wicked are cruel.

Lesson 18: Day 4

He who tills his land will be satisfied with bread,

But he who follows frivolity is devoid of understanding.

Proverbs 12:11 NKJV

Trace and Copy Key Words

satisfied

frivolity

devoid

Trace and copy the verse below.

He who tills his land

will be satisfied with bread,

But he who follows frivolity

is devoid of understanding.

Lesson 19: Day 1

The way of fools seems right to them,

but the wise listen to advice.

Proverbs 12:15 NIV

Trace and Copy Key Words

fools
listen
advice

Trace and copy the verse below.

The way of fools seems right to

them, but the wise listen to

advice.

Lesson 19: Day 2

Truthful lips endure forever,

but a lying tongue lasts only a moment.

Proverbs 12:19 NIV

Trace and Copy Key Words

truthful

endure

tongue

Trace and copy the verse below.

Truthful lips endure forever,

but a lying tongue lasts only a moment.

Truthful lips endure forever,

but a lying tongue lasts only a moment.

Lesson 19: Day 3

Trace and Copy Key Words

detests
delights
trustworthy

Trace and copy the verse below.

The LORD detests lying lips,

but he delights in people who are trustworthy.

Proverbs 12:22 NIV

Lesson 19: Day 4

Diligent hands will rule,

but laziness ends in forced labor.

Proverbs 12:24 NIV

Trace and Copy Key Words

diligent

rule

laziness

Trace and copy the verse below.

Diligent hands will rule,

but laziness ends in forced labor.

Diligent hands will rule,

but laziness ends in forced labor.

Lesson 20: Day 1

One who is righteous is a guide to his neighbor,
but the way of the wicked leads them astray.

Proverbs 12:26 ESV

Trace and Copy Key Words

guide
neighbor
astray

Trace and copy the verse below.

One who is righteous is

a guide to his neighbor,

but the way of the

wicked leads them astray.

Lesson 20: Day 2

A wise son hears his father's instruction,

but a scoffer does not listen to rebuke.

Proverbs 13:1 ESV

Trace and Copy Key Words

instruction

scoffer

rebuke

Trace and copy the verse below.

A wise son hears his father's instruction,

but a scoffer does not listen to rebuke.

Lesson 20: Day 3

Whoever guards his mouth preserves his life;

he who opens wide his lips comes to ruin.

Proverbs 13:3 ESV

Trace and Copy Key Words

guards

preserves

ruin

Trace and copy the verse below.

Whoever guards his mouth preserves his

life; he who opens wide his lips comes to

ruin.

Lesson 20: Day 4

The soul of the sluggard craves and gets nothing,

while the soul of the diligent is richly supplied.

Proverbs 13:4 ESV

Trace and Copy Key Words

sluggard

craves

diligent

Trace and copy the verse below.

The soul of the sluggard craves and gets nothing,

while the soul of the diligent is richly supplied.

Translating the Scriptures

Timeline of Bible Translation

(A.D. stands for *anno Domini*--"in the year of the Lord")

- **180 A.D.** The New Testament starts to be translated from Greek into Latin, Syriac, and Coptic.

- **195 A.D.** The name of the first translation of the Old and New Testaments into Latin was termed Old Latin, both Testaments having been translated from the Greek. Parts of the Old Latin were found in quotes by the church father Tertullian, who lived around 160-220 A.D. in north Africa and wrote treatises on theology.

- **300 A.D.** The Coptic Versions: Coptic was spoken in four dialects in Egypt. The Bible was translated into each of these four dialects.

- **300 A.D.** The Old Syriac was a translation of the New Testament from the Greek into Syriac.

- **380 A.D.** The Latin Vulgate was translated by St. Jerome. He translated into Latin the Old Testament from the Hebrew and the New Testament from Greek. The Latin Vulgate became the Bible of the Western Church until the Protestant Reformation in the 1500's. It continues to be the authoritative translation of the Roman Catholic Church to this day.

- **1380 A.D.** The first English translation of the Bible was by John Wycliffe. He translated the Bible into English from the Latin Vulgate. This was a translation from a translation and not a translation from the original Hebrew and Greek. Wycliffe was forced to translate from the Latin Vulgate because he did not know Hebrew or Greek.

- **1440s A. D.** Gutenberg invents the printing press and publishes the Gutenberg Bible in the Latin Vulgate.

- **1500s A.D.** The Protestant Reformation saw an increase in translations of the Bible into the common languages of the people.

- **1611 A.D.** The King James Bible, translated from Greek, Hebrew, and Aramaic, is completed by 47 scholars for the Church of England, and replaced the Wycliffe Bible as the official English translation of the Bible.

Copying the Scriptures

Most people in our country can read and many own several Bibles. But for a long time, it was very expensive to purchase a Bible. Also, very few people knew how to read. Therefore, few people owned a Bible. Can you imagine not being able to read your favorite book? That would be simply terrible. Some would say we are lucky, but really we are very blessed. If you ever feel like grumbling about your reading time, think about how many books you have. It might help you to have a change in your attitude.

In about 1456, a man named Johannes Gutenburg, invented the printing press. Wonder of wonders, something that used to take years to print by hand, letter by letter, could now be done very quickly on his printing press. That is when books started to become more available and less expensive. We can thank Mr. Gutenburg for making it possible for us to have all the books we want: easy books, hard books, books about math and science, and even books about your favorite games.

You can see very old copies of the Old and New Testaments in museums all around the world. This might be a fun field trip for you and your family to take.

Practicing Proverbs © 2016 Not to be reproduced.

87

Lesson 21: Day 1

There is that maketh himself rich, yet hath nothing:
there is that maketh himself poor, yet hath great riches.

Proverbs 13:7 KJV

Trace and Copy Key Words

maketh

nothing

riches

Trace and copy the verse below.

There is that maketh himself rich,

yet hath nothing;

there is that maketh himself poor,

yet hath great riches.

Lesson 21: Day 2

Only by pride cometh contention:

but with the well advised is wisdom.

Proverbs 13:10 KJV

Trace and Copy Key Words

pride

contention

advised

Trace and copy the verse below.

Only by pride cometh contention:

but with the well advised is wisdom.

Lesson 21: Day 3

Wealth gotten by vanity shall be diminished:
but he that gathereth by labour shall increase.

Proverbs 13:11 KJV

Trace and Copy Key Words

vanity
diminished
labour

Trace and copy the verse below.

Wealth gotten by vanity shall be diminished:

but he that gathereth by labour shall increase.

Lesson 21: Day 4

Every prudent man dealeth with knowledge:

but a fool layeth open his folly.

Proverbs 13:16 KJV

Trace and Copy Key Words

prudent

dealeth

folly

Trace and copy the verse below.

Every prudent man dealeth with knowledge:

but a fool layeth open his folly.

Every prudent man dealeth with knowledge:

but a fool layeth open his folly.

Lesson 22: Day 1

He who walks with wise men will be wise,

But the companion of fools will be destroyed.

Proverbs 13:20 NKJV

Trace and Copy Key Words

wise

companion

destroyed

Trace and copy the verse below.

He who walks with wise men will be wise,

But the companion of fools will be destroyed.

Lesson 22: Day 2

He who spares his rod hates his son,

But he who loves him disciplines him promptly.

Proverbs 13:24 NKJV

Trace and Copy Key Words

spares
disciplines
promptly

Trace and copy the verse below.

He who spares his rod hates his son,

But he who loves him disciplines him promptly.

Practicing Proverbs © 2016 Not to be reproduced.

Lesson 22: Day 3

A faithful witness does not lie,

But a false witness will utter lies.

Proverbs 14:5 NKJV

Trace and Copy Key Words

witness

faithful

false

Trace and copy the verse below.

A faithful witness

does not lie,

But a false witness will utter lies.

Lesson 22: Day 4

There is a way that seems right to a man,

But its end is the way of death.

Proverbs 14:12 NKJV

Trace and Copy Key Words

right

way

death

Trace and copy the verse below.

There is a way that seems right to a man,

But its end is the way of death.

There is a way that seems right to a man,

But its end is the way of death.

Lesson 23: Day 1

The simple believe anything,
but the prudent give thought to their steps.

Proverbs 14:15 NIV

Trace and Copy Key Words

simple

believe

thought

Trace and copy the verse below.

The simple believe anything,

but the prudent give thought to their steps.

Lesson 23: Day 2

Trace and Copy Key Words

foolish
devises
schemes

A quick-tempered person does foolish things,

and the one who devises evil schemes is hated.

Proverbs 14:17 NIV

Trace and copy the verse below.

A quick-tempered person does foolish things,

and the one who devises evil schemes is hated.

A quick-tempered person does foolish things,

and the one who devises evil schemes is hated.

Lesson 23: Day 3

The simple inherit folly,

but the prudent are crowned with knowledge.

Proverbs 14:18 NIV

Trace and Copy Key Words

inherit

crowned

prudent

Trace and copy the verse below.

The simple inherit folly,

but the prudent are crowned with

knowledge.

Lesson 23: Day 4

Trace and Copy Key Words

despise

blessed

needy

It is a sin to despise one's neighbor,
but blessed is the one who is kind to the needy.

Proverbs 14:21 NI

Trace and copy the verse below.

It is a sin to despise one's neighbor,

but blessed is the one who is kind to the needy.

Practicing Proverbs © 2016 Not to be reproduced.

Lesson 24: Day 1

In all toil there is profit,
but mere talk tends only to poverty.
Proverbs 14:23 ESV

Trace and Copy Key Words

toil
profit
poverty

Trace and copy the verse below.

In all toil there is profit,

but mere talk tends only to poverty.

Lesson 24: Day 2

In the fear of the LORD one has strong confidence,

and his children will have a refuge.

Proverbs 14:26 ESV

Trace and Copy Key Words

confidence

children

refuge

Trace and copy the verse below.

In the fear of the LORD

one has strong confidence,

and his children

will have a refuge.

Lesson 24: Day 3

Whoever is slow to anger has great understanding,

but he who has a hasty temper exalts folly.

Proverbs 14:29 ESV

Trace and Copy Key Words

anger
hasty
great
temper

Trace and copy the verse below.

Whoever is slow to anger has great understanding,

but he who has a hasty temper exalts folly.

Lesson 24: Day 4

Trace and Copy Key Words

soft
wrath
Rahab

A soft answer turns away wrath,
but a harsh word stirs up anger.

Proverbs 15:1 ESV

Trace and copy the verse below.

A soft answer turns away wrath,

but a harsh word stirs up anger.

A soft answer turns away wrath,

but a harsh word stirs up anger.

Lesson 25: Day 1

The eyes of the LORD are in every place,
beholding the evil and the good.
Proverbs 15:3 KJV

Trace and Copy Key Words

beholding

evil

good

Trace and copy the verse below.

The eyes of the LORD are in every place,

beholding the evil and the good.

Lesson 25: Day 2

A fool despiseth his father's instruction:

but he that regardeth reproof is prudent.

Proverbs 15:5 KJV

Trace and Copy Key Words

instruction
regardeth
reproof

Trace and copy the verse below.

A fool despiseth his father's instruction:

but he that regardeth reproof is prudent.

A fool despiseth his father's instruction:

but he that regardeth reproof is prudent.

Lesson 25: Day 3

A merry heart maketh a cheerful countenance: but by sorrow of the heart the spirit is broken.

Proverbs 15:13 KJV

Trace and Copy Key Words

merry
cheerful
countenance

Trace and copy the verse below.

A merry heart maketh a cheerful
countenance: but by sorrow of
the heart the spirit is broken.

Lesson 25: Day 4

Better is little with the fear of the LORD
than great treasure and trouble therewith.

Proverbs 15:16 KJV

Trace and Copy Key Words

better.

treasure

trouble

Trace and copy the verse below.

Better is little with the fear of the LORD

than great treasure and trouble therewith.

Better is little with the fear of the LORD

than great treasure and trouble therewith.

Lesson 26: Day 1

Better is a dinner of herbs where love is,

Than a fatted calf with hatred.

Proverbs 15:17 NKJV

Trace and Copy Key Words

herbs
fatted
of

Trace and copy the verse below.

Better is a dinner of herbs where love is,

Than a fatted calf with hatred.

Lesson 26: Day 2

The heart of the righteous studies how to answer,

But the mouth of the wicked pours forth evil.

Proverbs 15:28 NKJV

Trace and Copy Key Words

studies

answer

wicked

Trace and copy the verse below.

The heart of the righteous studies to answer,

But the mouth of the wicked pours forth evil.

The heart of the righteous studies to answer,

But the mouth of the wicked pours forth evil.

Lesson 26: Day 3

The LORD is far from the wicked,
But He hears the prayer of the righteous.
Proverbs 15:29 NKJV

Trace and Copy Key Words

prayer
righteous

Trace and copy the verse below.

The LORD is far from the wicked,
But He hears the prayer of the righteous.

Lesson 26: Day 4

The fear of the LORD is the instruction of wisdom,

And before honor is humility.

Proverbs 15:33 NKJV

Trace and Copy Key Words

instruction

honor

humility

Trace and copy the verse below.

The fear of the LORD

is the instruction of wisdom,

And before honor

is humility.

Practicing Proverbs © 2016 Not to be reproduced.

Lesson 27: Day 1

All a person's ways seem pure to them,
but motives are weighed by the LORD.

Proverbs 16:2 NIV

Trace and Copy Key Words

pure
motives
weighed

Trace and copy the verse below.

All a person's ways seem pure to them,

but motives are weighed by the LORD.

Lesson 27: Day 2

Trace and Copy Key Words

commit
establish
plans

Commit to the LORD whatever you do,

and he will establish your plans.

Proverbs 16:3 NIV

Trace and copy the verse below.

Commit to the LORD establish your plans,

Commit to the LORD establish your plans,

Lesson 27: Day 3

When the LORD takes pleasure in anyone's way,
he causes their enemies to make peace with them.

Proverbs 16:7 NIV

Trace and Copy Key Words

pleasure
enemies
peace

Trace and copy the verse below.

When the LORD takes pleasure in anyone's way,

he causes their enemies to make peace with them.

Lesson 27: Day 4

In their hearts humans plan their course,

but the LORD establishes their steps.

Proverbs 1:8 KJV

Trace and Copy Key Words

hearts

humans

course

Trace and copy the verse below.

In their hearts humans plan their course,

but the LORD establishes their steps.

In their hearts humans plan their course,

but the LORD establishes their steps.

Lesson 28: Day 1

How much better to get wisdom than gold!

To get understanding is to be chosen rather than silver.

Proverbs 16:16 ESV

Trace and Copy Key Words

wisdom

gold

silver

Trace and copy the verse below.

How much better

to get wisdom than

to get understanding

to be chosen rather than silver.

Lesson 28: Day 2

Pride goes before destruction,

and a haughty spirit before a fall.

Proverbs 16:18 ESV

Trace and Copy Key Words

Pride

haughty

spirit

Trace and copy the verse below.

Pride goes before destruction,

and a haughty spirit before a fall.

Pride goes before destruction,

and a haughty spirit before a fall.

Lesson 28: Day 3

Gracious words are like a honeycomb,
sweetness to the soul and health to the body.

Proverbs 16:24 ESV

Trace and Copy Key Words

gracious
honeycomb
sweetness

Trace and copy the verse below.

Gracious words are like a honeycomb,

sweetness to the soul and health to the

body.

Lesson 28: Day 4

Trace and Copy Key Words

seems
right
death

There is a way that seems right to a man,

but its end is the way to death.

Proverbs 16:25 ESV

Trace and copy the verse below.

There is a way that seems right to a man,

but its end is the way to death.

There is a way that seems right to a man,

but its end is the way to death.

Lesson 29: Day 1

He that is slow to anger is better than the mighty;
and he that ruleth his spirit than he that taketh a city.

Proverbs 16:32 KJV

Trace and Copy Key Words

mighty

ruleth

taketh

Trace and copy the verse below.

He that is slow to anger

is better than the mighty,

and he that ruleth his spirit

than he that taketh a city.

Lesson 29: Day 2

Better is a dry morsel, and quietness therewith,

than an house full of sacrifices with strife.

Proverbs 17:1 KJV

Trace and Copy Key Words

morsel

sacrifices

strife

Trace and copy the verse below.

Better is a dry morsel, and quietness therewith,

than an house full of sacrifices with strife.

Better is a dry morsel, and quietness therewith,

than an house full of sacrifices with strife.

Lesson 29: Day 3

Children's children are the crown of old men;
and the glory of children are their fathers.

Proverbs 17:6 KJV

Trace and Copy Key Words

children

crown

fathers

Trace and copy the verse below.

Children's children are the crown of old men;

and the glory of children are their fathers.

Lesson 29: Day 4

Trace and Copy Key Words

bear
rather
wrathful

Let a bear robbed of her whelps meet a man,

rather than a fool in his folly.

Proverbs 17:12 KJV

Trace and copy the verse below.

Let a bear robbed of her whelps meet a man,

rather than a fool in his folly.

Let a bear robbed of her whelps meet a man,

rather than a fool in his folly.

Lesson 30: Day 1

A merry heart does good, like medicine,
But a broken spirit dries the bones.
Proverbs 17:22 NKJV

Trace and Copy Key Words

heart
medicine
broken

Trace and copy the verse below.

a merry heart does good, like medicine,

but a broken spirit dries the bones

Lesson 30: Day 2

A foolish son is a grief to his father,

And bitterness to her who bore him.

Proverbs 17:25 NKJV

Trace and Copy Key Words

grief

bitterness

bore

Trace and copy the verse below.

A foolish son is a grief to his father,

And bitterness to her who bore him.

A foolish son is a grief to his father,

And bitterness to her who bore him.

Lesson 30: Day 3

A fool's mouth is his destruction,
And his lips are the snare of his soul.
Proverbs 18:7 NKJV

Trace and Copy Key Words

fool

snare

soul

Trace and copy the verse below.

A fool's mouth is his destruction,

And his lips are the snare of his soul.

Lesson 30: Day 4

He who is slothful in his work

Is a brother to him who is a great destroyer.

Proverbs 18:9 NKJV

Trace and Copy Key Words

slothful

brother

destroyer

Trace and copy the verse below.

He who is slothful in his work

Is a brother to him who is a great destroyer.

Items Available from Laurelwood Books

Ōlim, Once Upon a Time, in Latin Series

Readers and Workbooks
(Supplementary audio files available for all Latin titles)

Book I: *The Three Little Pigs, The Tortoise and the Hare, The Crow and the Pitcher*
Book II: *The Ant and the Chrysalis, The Lost Sheep, The Good Samaritan*
Book III: *The Feeding of the 5,000, The Lion and the Mouse*
Book IV: *Creation*
Book V: *Daniel, Part I; We Know a Tree by its Fruit*
Book VI: *The Prodigal Son*
Book VII: *David and Goliath*
Book VIII: *Daniel, Part II*
Book IX: *Daniel, Part III, The Miser*
Book X: *The Wise Man and Foolish Man, The Ten Maidens*

Ōlim Derivatives I, II
Latin Verbs: To Infinitives and Beyond! Book I, II, III
Latin for Littles, Vol I

Scripture Scribes Series

Pre-Primary: *From Scribbler to Scribe*

Primary: *Who Made Me?, My Whole Heart, His Name Is Wonderful, Psalms & Proverbs for Young Catholics, Practicing Proverbs, Following Jesus with Scripture, Song, and Art*

Intermediate: *One Another, Savoring Psalms, Foundations of Faith*

Upper School: *Men of Honor & Women of Grace, Walking With God*

Extra Practice Workbooks: Primary, Intermediate
(For use with Patriotic Penmanship and Scripture Scribes)

Items available from Laurelwood Books

Patriotic Penmanship Series

Grades K-6
Junior High, Book I & II
Senior High, Book I & II

With Unique Titles:
    Grade 4 for Lefties
    Grade 6 Enlarged Script
    Dinosaurs From A to Z Manuscript Review Book
    Transition to Cursive Book
    Jump Rope Cursive Review Book

Study Guides

Based on Rosemary Sutcliff's historical fiction:
    The Eagle of the Ninth
    The Silver Branch
    Outcast
    The Lantern Bearers
    Warrior Scarlet
    Sword Song
    The Shining Company

Based on Emma Leslie's historical fiction:
    Out of the Mouth of the Lion
    Glaucia the Greek Slave

State The Facts: A Guide to Studying Your State
    This book offers your student the opportunity to research
    and learn state history, geography, weather, and more!

Laurelwood Books offers both new and used curricula to families wishing to help their children learn and achieve success in school or at home.

To order: www.laurelwoodbooks.com
Books@Laurelwoodbooks.com

Made in the USA
Monee, IL
08 May 2020